Earth-Friendly CRAFTS

CLEVER WAYS TO REUSE EVERYDAY ITEMS

KATHY ROSS · Illustrated by **CÉLINE MALÉPART**

M Millbrook Press · Minneapolis

For Maia!
— KR

 This symbol appears next to materials that can be reused to make the crafts in this book.

All cover and interior images in this book are used with the permission of:
Crafts photographed by Todd Strand/ Independent Picture Service; background photo
of grass and clouds used throughout book: © iStockphoto.com/Nadezda Firsova.

Millbrook Press
A division of Lerner Publishing Group, Inc.
241 First Avenue North
Minneapolis, MN 55401 U.S.A.

Website address: www.lernerbooks.com

Library of Congress Cataloging-in-Publication Data

Ross, Kathy (Katharine Reynolds), 1948–
    Earth-friendly crafts : clever ways to reuse everyday items / by Kathy Ross ;
illustrated by Céline Malépart.
        p.   cm.
    ISBN: 978-0-8225-9099-6 (lib. bdg. : alk. paper)
        1. Handicraft–Juvenile literature. 2. Recycling (Waste, etc.)–Juvenile
literature. I. Malépart, Céline, ill. II. Title.
    TT160.R71422953 2009
      745.5–dc22   2008025481

Manufactured in the United States of America

1 2 3 4 5 6 – BP – 14 13 12 11 10 09

CONTENTS

Materials:

- tiny figurine or toy
- craft jewels, tiny flowers, or other collage items
- thin craft ribbon
- eyelash yarn
- ruler
- scissors
- white craft glue

Steps:

1 Glue collage items to the tiny figurine or toy to decorate it and hide any damage. Let dry.

2 Cut one 3-foot (0.9-m) length each of craft ribbon and eyelash yarn.

3 Hold the yarn and ribbon together.

4 Fold in half. Glue the fold to the bottom of the figure so the ends hang down. Let dry.

5 Trim the ends so they are even.

Small toys and figurines, even when chipped, cracked, or fading, make charming bookmarks.

Picture Board

Materials:

- ♻ old bath scrubby, washed and dried
- ♻ box with lid 5 to 8 inches (13 to 20 cm) wide
- ♻ cereal box
- ♻ small pictures from greeting cards, magazines, or catalogs
- pipe cleaner
- craft paint
- paintbrush
- masking tape
- scissors
- white craft glue

Steps:

1 If the lid has writing on it, paint the top and sides. Let dry.

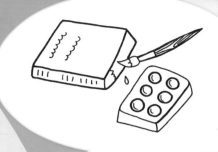

2 Cut off the scrubby rope. You will have a long net tube. Cut a piece that is two and a half times the length of the box lid.

3 Slide the lid into the center of the tube. Tie the two net ends together under the lid so that the net is snug.

4 Cut out the small pictures. Glue them to the cereal box cardboard. Let dry. Cut out the cardboard-backed pictures.

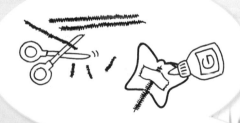

5 Cut a piece of pipe cleaner for each picture. Glue one end to the back of the picture. Secure with tape.

6 Slip the non-glued ends through the net. Arrange the pictures to create a scene. Put the lid on the box. Stand the box and lid on its side to display.

Add to your picture collection over time. You can create different pictures for different times of the year. Stash the extra pictures inside the box.

Designer Car Clip

Materials:

- ♻ old, small (3 inches, or 8 cm) toy car
- ♻ clamp clothespin
- metallic trim, craft jewels and beads, or other collage items
- craft paint
- paintbrush
- ♻ newspaper
- white craft glue

Steps:

1

Clean the toy car.
Let dry.

2

Working on the newspaper, paint
the car and the clothespin. Let dry.

3

Decorate the car using the collage items.
Craft jewels are perfect to glue over
wheels or to replace missing ones.

4

Glue the bottom of the car to
the clothespin.

Even damaged cars work for
this project!

Marker Caps Pencil Holder

Materials:

- 25 to 30 fat marker caps
- tuna-fish-type can, clean and dry
- single sock
- felt or fleece scrap
- collage materials
- ribbon
- ruler
- pencil
- scissors
- white craft glue

Steps:

1 Cover the inside of the can with a thin layer of glue. Place the marker caps inside, open ends up. Let dry.

2 Slide the sock cuff over the can. Glue the sock to the outside of the can. Let dry.

3 Cut off the sock about 1 inch (2.5 cm) below the bottom of the can. Glue the excess sock to the bottom. Let dry.

4 Trace the can's outline onto the felt or fleece. Cut out the circle, and glue it to the bottom of the can.

5 Glue ribbon trim around the top edge.

6 Decorate with collage materials.

Recycled steel cans, like tuna fish cans, can be made into cars, girders for buildings, or new food cans.

Changing Faces Necklace

Materials:

 **small clear plastic toy capsule from vending machine**

small beads, sequins, craft jewels, or other collage items

two 1½-inch (3.8-cm) pom-poms

½-inch (1.3-cm) pom-pom

toothpick

thin craft ribbon

ruler

scissors

white craft glue

Steps:

1 Place one large pom-pom in the capsule for a face and a second one on top for hair.

2 Select items from the collage materials to create a face.

3 Use the toothpick to help place the items inside the capsule, between the face pom-pom and the capsule.

4 Place the lid back on the capsule. Glue the small pom-pom to the center of the lid. Let dry.

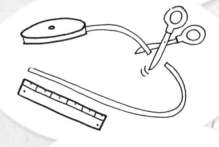

5 Cut a 2-foot (0.6-m) length of the ribbon.

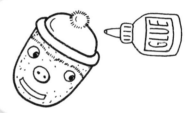

6 Tuck an end into each side of the capsule. Snap the lid shut.

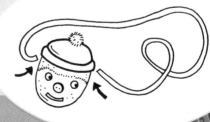

To give the necklace a new look, just change the collage items inside!

Box Board Links

Materials:

- ♻ cereal boxes or greeting cards
- ♻ playing card
- pencil
- ruler
- scissors
- white craft glue

Steps:

1 Trace around the playing card on the cereal box or greeting card. Cut out the shape.

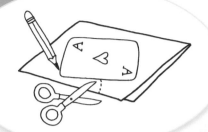

2 Cut another piece of cardboard of similar size.

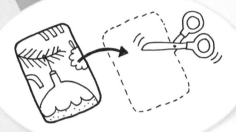

3 Glue the outer edges of the two pieces together with the colored sides out. Let dry.

4 On a long side, cut about ¹/₂ inch (1.3 cm) into the center. Then cut ¹/₂ inch from the outside all the way around to remove the center portion. This creates one link.

5 Make a chain of links by slipping one link through the cut opening of another link.

Remember to recyle the leftover scraps of greeting cards or cereal boxes with your paper recycling!

Beaded Picture Boxes

Materials:

- box with a lid
- small pictures from greeting cards, magazines, or catalogs
- seed and bugle beads
- craft jewels
- craft paint
- paintbrush
- ribbons, trim
- Styrofoam tray
- scissors
- white craft glue

Steps:

1 Cut out the pictures.

2 Working on the Styrofoam tray, glue beads to the picture to decorate it.

3 Use craft jewels to accent some parts of the picture. Let dry.

4 If the box has writing on it, you will need to paint it first. Let dry.

5 Glue the picture to the lid of the box.

6 Glue trim around the edges of the box lid. Let dry.

You could also decorate a large box and use it to store your recyclable materials.

Necktie Clown Pin

Materials:

- ♻ old necktie
- ♻ three ½-inch (1.3-cm) pom-poms
- ♻ rickrack or trim
- two wiggle eyes
- red pipe cleaner
- safety pin
- ruler
- scissors
- white craft glue

Steps:

1 Cut a 3-inch (8-cm) piece from the narrow end of the necktie.

2 Glue a piece of rickrack or trim across the tie as shown. Glue a pom-pom to the tip.

3 Snip some fuzz from the sides of a pom-pom. Glue it below the trim and on the two sides of the tie.

4 Glue on the two wiggle eyes. Glue on a pom-pom below the eyes.

5 Cut a small piece of pipe cleaner. Curve it into a smile. Glue it on.

6 Glue rickrack or trim along the bottom of the tie. Attach the safety pin to the back.

You can also make a clown hand puppet from the wide end of the tie using this same design.

Coloring Book Collage

Materials:

- ♻ used coloring book
- ♻ cereal box cardboard
- fabric and felt scraps
- trim or ribbon
- beads, gems, tiny flowers, or other collage material
- pins
- pencil
- ruler
- scissors
- white craft glue

Steps:

1 Carefully rip out a page from a coloring book. Trace the page onto the cereal box cardboard. Cut it out.

2 Cover one side of the cardboard with felt cut to the same size. Glue it on. Let dry.

3 Cut out the main shape of the coloring page. Cut out any smaller shapes too. Pin the shapes to a piece of fabric. Cut out the shapes from the fabric.

4 Glue the main shape to the felt-covered cardboard. Glue on the smaller shapes.

5 Glue on the trim, gems, beads, and other collage materials.

6 Cut a 2-foot (0.6-m) piece of ribbon. Glue the two ends of the ribbon to the back of the collage.

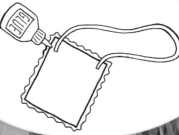

Old clothes, used wrapping paper, and broken jewelry are all great things to save for this project.

Glove Octopus Puppet

Materials:

- two stretchy gloves
- two colors of craft foam
- pipe cleaner
- ruler
- scissors
- white craft glue

Steps:

1 Turn the thumb of each glove inside itself.

2 Hold the two gloves together with the short fingers on opposite ends.

3 Fold one cuff down over the cuff of the second glove to form a head.

4 Cut eyes from one color of foam. Cut pupils from the other color. Glue them to the head.

5 Cut a 1½-inch (3.8-cm) piece of pipe cleaner. Shape it into a smile, and glue the smile on. Let dry.

To use the puppet, slip your fingers into the folded-down cuff at the back of the head.

Puzzle Pieces
Alligator

Materials:

- old jigsaw puzzle
- plastic grocery bag
- two large wiggle eyes
- two green pony beads
- white craft glue

Steps:

1 Choose puzzle pieces of similar color. Place the plastic bag on a flat surface.

2 Working on the plastic bag, make an outline of an alligator with puzzle pieces. Fill in the outline with more pieces.

3 Glue overlapping puzzle pieces on top of the alligator shape. Keep adding glue and pieces until you like how it looks.

4 Glue two puzzle pieces sticking out on each side of the body.

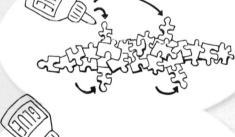

5 Glue the two pony beads to the head.

6 Stand the two wiggle eyes in front of the beads. Glue them down. Let dry.

Instead of using plastic or paper bags to carry your groceries home, bring a reusable bag to the store.

Balloon Bird Magnet

Materials:

- two deflated latex round balloons, different colors
- flat cap, such as a milk jug cap
- pom-pom that fits inside cap
- two wiggle eyes
- sticky-back magnet
- scissors
- white craft glue

Steps:

1 Cut the neck off one of the balloons, leaving a point.

2 Slip the cap inside the balloon.

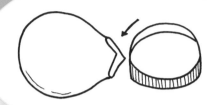

3 Slip the pom-pom inside the balloon so the pom-pom sits in the cap.

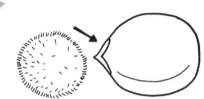

4 Cut a triangle beak from the second balloon. Glue it over the point at the neck.

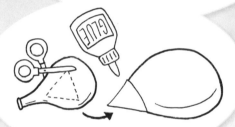

5 Glue on the wiggle eyes.

6 Press a piece of sticky-back magnet to the back of the bird's head.

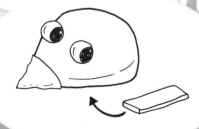

Here's another fun balloon craft: Fill a round balloon with rice or dried lentils. Tie the end off, and put on three more balloon layers. Now you've made a juggling ball!

Stand-up Frame

Materials:

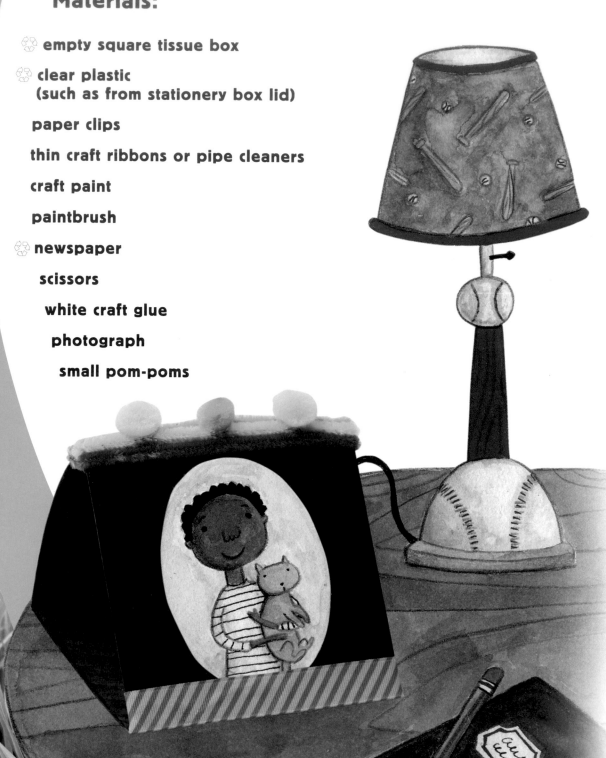

- ♻ empty square tissue box
- ♻ clear plastic (such as from stationery box lid)
- paper clips
- thin craft ribbons or pipe cleaners
- craft paint
- paintbrush
- ♻ newspaper
- scissors
- white craft glue
- photograph
- small pom-poms

Steps:

1 Carefully take apart the seams of the box so it is a flat piece of cardboard. Remove the cellophane insert.

2 Cut off the entire end flap and the two side flaps from the end opposite the oval opening.

3 Working on newspaper, paint one side of the remaining flat box. Let dry. Paint the other side.

4 Cut a square from the plastic to fit over the oval opening. Glue the edges of the plastic to the back of the opening. Let dry.

5 Glue the two side flaps together over the back of the opening. Let dry. Slip a photo into the frame, behind the plastic.

6 Glue the tab at the oval end to the edge of the opposite end. Secure with paper clips until the glue dries.

7 Tie craft ribbon in a bow around the top of the frame, or attach pipe cleaners and pom-poms for decoration.

Newspapers can be recycled up to seven times! They are made into more newspapers.

Changing Faces Pin

Materials:

- ♻ 3-inch (8-cm) round metal slogan pin
- collage items
- sticky-back magnet strip
- craft paint
- paintbrush
- ♻ newspaper
- hole punch
- scissors

Steps:

1 Working on newspaper, paint the front of the metal button. Let dry.

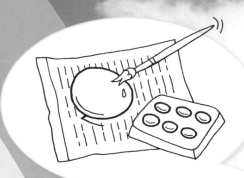

2 Punch holes from the sticky-back magnet strip for each collage item. Use scissors to cut larger magnet pieces, if needed.

3 Attach the sticky side of a magnet piece to each collage item. Bigger items will require bigger pieces of magnet.

4 Design a face using the collage items.

5 Mix up the pieces to make different faces.

Slogan pins are made of copper, plastic, paper, and steel. Did you know that steel can be recycled again and again?

Slinky CD Holder

Materials:

- old slinky
- damaged CD
- thin craft ribbon
- artificial flower
- scissors
- white craft glue

Steps:

1

Bring the two ends of the slinky together.

2

Tie the ends together with two pieces of ribbon. Secure with glue.

3

Glue the slinky to the center of the silver side of the CD. Let dry.

4

You can leave the holder plain or glue a flower in the center to decorate it.

How about using old CDs as coasters? Just glue some fabric or felt to both sides.

Royal Jewelry

Materials:

- king and queen playing cards
- clear glass 1-inch (2.5-cm) plant gems
- felt scraps
- gold trim, seed beads, and sequins
- gold cord
- permanent markers
- pin-backs
- sticky-back magnet strip
- ruler
- scissors
- white craft glue
- pencil

Steps:

1 Cut the king or queen from the card. You can include the robe or cut out just the head.

2 Use markers to add color to the hair and face.

3 Decorate the crown and robe with bits of gold trim, beads, and sequins. Glue a glass plant gem over the face. Make a crown and glue it to the head. Let dry.

4 Trace the figure onto the felt. Cut out the felt. Glue it to the back of the figure.

5 If you are making a necklace, glue the two ends of a 2-foot (0.6-m) gold cord between the felt and the figure.

6 To make a pin, glue a pin-back on the back. To make a magnet, press a piece of sticky-back magnet on the back.

Using old playing cards, you can make jewelry fit for royalty.

Game Board Art Folder

Materials:

- ♻ folding game board (make sure it's a game you don't use anymore)
- ♻ printed wrapping paper
- wide ribbon
- ruler
- scissors
- white craft glue
- collage items

Steps:

1 Glue the wrapping paper to the inside of the game board. Make sure the board will open and fold without tearing the paper. Let dry.

2 Cut a 3- to 4-foot (0.9- to 1.2-m) piece of ribbon.

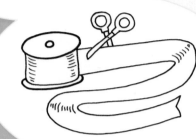

3 Glue the ribbon across the back of the folded board so equal lengths of ribbon are hanging off to the sides. Let dry.

4 Tie the ribbon in a bow, and trim the ends, if needed.

5 Decorate the outside of the folder with collage items, pictures from cards and magazines or, better yet, your own art!

You can use this folder to keep your artwork protected and flat.

Hairbrush Hair Clip Holder

Materials:

- old plastic hairbrush, clean and dry
- pony beads
- seed beads
- ½-inch (1.3-cm) wide ribbon
- 12-inch (30-cm) sparkle stem
- ruler
- scissors
- white craft glue

Steps:

1 Cut two 3-foot (0.9-m) pieces of ribbon.

2 Tie a ribbon around each brush end. Let the ribbon ends hang down.

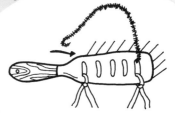

3 Hook the two ends of the sparkle stem through the top of the brush or the bristles to form a hanger.

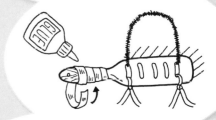

4 Cover the handle with glue, and wrap it with ribbon. Trim off any extra ribbon once the handle is covered.

5 Write a word or your name on the handle with glue and seed beads. Let dry.

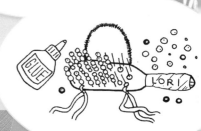

6 Cover the bristles of the brush with glue and layers of colorful pony beads. Let dry.

Hang the colorful hairbrush on your wall, and clip barrettes and hair clips to the ribbons to organize them.

Fashionable Note Card & Envelope

Materials:

- small doll outfit
- used greeting card
- fabric or wrapping paper
- light-colored construction paper
- thin ribbon
- sequins, trim, or other collage materials
- hole punch
- scissors
- white craft glue

Steps to make the card:

1 Glue plain paper to the inside of the card to cover up any writing. Let dry.

2 Glue fabric or wrapping paper onto the front of the card. Glue on the doll outfit. Let dry.

3 Decorate the dress using the collage materials.

Steps to make the envelope:

1 Fold a piece of construction paper in half. Trim the sides wider than the card. Glue two sides together. Let dry.

2 Punch two holes through the top of the open side.

3 Thread a piece of ribbon through the holes, and tie in a bow to close.

If you unwrap a present carefully, you can wrap another gift with the paper. You can also use the paper to make cards, envelopes, or other fun things!

Display Bird

Materials:

♻ **wood or plastic paddle from paddle ball game**

12-inch (30-cm) orange pipe cleaner

wiggle eye

orange felt scrap

craft feather

thin craft ribbon

paper clip

ruler

scissors

white craft glue

Hannah,
Please put
out the
recycling
♡ Love, Dad

Gree
BAG

Steps:

1 Fold the felt scrap in half. Cut a triangle beak on the fold. Glue the fold of the beak on the edge of the handle of the paddle.

2 Glue on the wiggle eye. Glue on a craft feather for a wing. Let dry.

3 Fold the pipe cleaner in half. Cut an inch off each end. Wrap a piece around each end of the pipe cleaner to shape the feet.

4 Glue the pipe cleaner fold to the back of the paddle so that the feet hang down. Let dry.

5 Cut a 12-inch (30-cm) piece of the craft ribbon. Glue the two ends on the back of the paddle. Let dry.

6 Cut a second piece of the craft ribbon. Thread the paper clip onto the ribbon. Tie the ribbon in a bow around the neck. Trim the ends, if needed.

To use the bird, hang it up and slip a favorite card, photo, or A+ paper in the paper clip to display.

Art Cards

Materials:

- old playing cards
- fabric scraps
- wrapping paper, newspaper, or brown bag paper
- copy of a photo
- pictures and words cut from old cards, magazines, or catalogs
- buttons, sequins, craft gems, trim, pieces of old jewelry, or other collage materials
- white craft glue
- scissors

Steps:

1 Cut two pieces of paper or fabric the size of the playing card. Glue pieces to both sides of the playing card. Let dry.

2 Glue on a copy of a photo of you or any other image that catches your eye.

3 Look in old magazines to find a word you like or a word that describes you. Cut out the letters to spell it. Glue onto your card.

4 Have fun decorating each card in your own unique style, using your favorite collage materials. The possibilities are endless!

Get together with your friends and make art cards to keep or to trade. Be sure to sign your name on each of your creations.

Resources

WEBSITES

Clean Sweep U.S.A.
http://www.cleansweepusa.org
This site offers three Web comics with information about waste management, littering, and beautification.

Energy Kids Page
http://www.eia.doe.gov/kids
This site from the U.S. Department of Energy includes energy facts, energy history, riddles, puzzles, and more.

Keep America Beautiful Kids' Zone
http://www.kab.org/kids_zone
Tips on how to keep the United States beautiful and a recycling game are available on this site.

BOOKS

Donald, Rhonda Lucas. *Recycling.* Danbury, CT: Children's Press, 2002.

Elliot, Marion. *Fun with Recycling: 50 Great Things for Kids to Make from Junk.* London: Southwater, 2001.

Gibbons, Gail. *Recycle!: A Handbook for Kids.* New York: Little, Brown and Company, 1996.

Harlow, Rosie. *Garbage and Recycling.* New York: Kingfisher Books, 2002.

Lewis, Barbara A. *The Kid's Guide to Service Projects: Over 500 Service Ideas for Young People Who Want to Make a Difference.* Edited by Pamela Espeland. Minneapolis: Free Spirit Publishing, 1995.

Martin, Laura C. *Recycled Crafts Box.* North Adams, MA: Storey Publishing, 2004.

Wilcox, Charlotte. *Recycling.* Minneapolis: Lerner Publications Company, 2007.

TIPS FOR KIDS

* Don't litter.
* Bring unwanted clothes to a local thrift shop.
* Make sure trash can lids are on tight before setting cans by the curb.
* Make litterbags for your parents' cars and for your bicycle.
* If your school's playground doesn't have a trash can, ask a teacher to see if the school will put one out.
* Ask your teacher to take the class on a field trip to a recycling center or a sanitary landfill.
* Whenever you go to a park or a beach, take a litterbag with you for your own trash in case you can't find a public trash can.
* Ask a teacher to invite your city's park maintenance person to speak to your class about the importance of not littering.
* While enjoying a park or any open space, hike on designated trails only, don't pick rare flowers or plants, and don't disturb the wild animals.
* Volunteer to help organize a cleanup at your school, your city, or your neighborhood.
* To learn more about recycling in your area, call your city or county.
* Check out your state's Adopt a Highway program.

STATISTICS*

* The amount of trash Americans created was reduced from 248 million tons in 2004 to 246 million tons in 2005.
* Of that, 79 million tons were recycled or composted.
* Container and packaging recycling increased 40 percent.
* Sixty-two percent of yard waste was composted.
* Fifty percent of all paper products were recycled— about 42 million tons.

*United States Recycling Statistics from http://greenliving.lovetoknow.com/ United_States_Recycling_Statistics. From the United States Environmental Protection Agency

A Note from Kathy Ross

One of the good things you can do for our planet is to not waste things. Reusing our resources instead of throwing them away is good for our Earth. Ever since I was a young child, I have loved to take what other people throw away and turn it into something useful. It seems as if the more I do it, the more ideas I have.

This is a book of project ideas for making new things out of what other people discard. It is intended to give you some sense of the tremendous possibilities for fun while giving unwanted objects new life as useful and artistic items. It is my hope that my ideas will inspire even more ideas of your own.

Look around your house, and see how many good sturdy items get tossed out on a regular basis. Start a collection box for the items needed for the projects in this book and other things you think you might be able to craft into something else. Have fun and help our planet at the same time!

–Kathy Ross

About the Author

With more than one million copies of her books in print, Kathy Ross has written over fifty titles and her name has become synonymous with "top quality craft books." Following twenty-five years of developing nursery school programs and guiding young children through craft projects, Ross has authored many successful series, including Crafts for Kids Who Are Learning about..., Girl Crafts, and All New Holiday Crafts for Kids.